IF MY WINDOWS COULD SPEAK

Athira Radhakrishnan

India | USA | UK

Presentation by *BookLeaf Publishing*

Web: www.bookleafpub.com

E-mail: info@bookleafpub.com

ISBN: 9789360948177

First edition 2024

*To one of my favourite strangers, you inspired
me to write again. Thanks*

ACKNOWLEDGEMENT

Many thanks to my best friend, brother, nephew, family, friends and a number of people for always being there for me. I can not show my gratitude to only one because I have many kind-hearted friends.
They make me keep going. Thanks a lot

I would not be able to write any of the poems without love. Thanks to a few who were my lovers. Thank you for the love.

Once again thanks to all of my friends.

PREFACE

All the midnight thoughts became my poems.
After a long day, my soul could not sleep, The
layers of my emotions peeled at all night. I
believe, poets never sleep properly until they
give birth to poems.
I heard someone say, that when people can
convert their emotions into poems then they are
blessed. Those words make me think I am
blessed. If I did not care about my emotions then
I could not make this.

My Scotch Pie

A good scran was waiting on the table
Mac and Cheese didn't say cheese to me
Chicken fillets couldn't fill my gut
Oh, Haddock had no head
I saw haggis, neeps and tatties,
Thegither say nae to me

There I saw someone hid
Inside the baps
Oh, that's a cute Scotch pie
My gut rumbled twice
But my hand hung back for a sec
Oh, Scotch pie
You are my downfall
I finished it in one gulp
I grinned like a Cheshire Cat

She Was Right

She was right
I dreamed under the dark sky
In the place, stars couldn't shine
I walked on the foggy road
In the path, the Mist made me blind
I swam in the sea of tears
On my way, lost my energy

She was right
I fell for the distant star,
But this star never knew
My dream, my blindness
And my tears were for her.
Now I experienced metanoia
And she was not right.

Day Off

The day begins with
a glimmer of light
slippery feet
gloomy mind

walking in an upside room
clock ticking for nothing
windows open for breathing
mirror smiles for doubting
and I am
grateful for nothing

Someone I Used To Know

I would be the Harpy
I would be an Anemoi
I would be a Poseidon
I would be a Zeus
And I would do anything
Only if you asked me to

I have been thinking
Since the day we parted
I have been reminiscing about
The words you displayed to me
I have been dying
Since the chaos started
Merking my heart.

Perhaps, I am a brainless
But you become a heartless
Perhaps, I am a snowflake
But you become a tepid
Perhaps, I am a lovesick
But you become an untruthful
At last, we become strangers
Aren't we?

Unknown Child

A toddler stepped on the land
Where the sun never shined
Happiness hid in a locker
Somebody left the key
Again and again went
Behind the key
Never found

A quarter century of nullity
A young adult never experienced
Homesickness
Wrathfulness became a nuclear bomb
Wandered into an unstable passion
Diffidence and sadness
Emotions tied together
Till I draw the last breath
As an unknown child.

A Love Letter On The Fire

The great ocean waves were her curves
As she moved
She owned the entire world
Those wild nights
She became a fire
As she moved I burned my entire body
Without asking a word
I became a slave to her eyes

My longings whispered
She is the one
Her fabulous form told me
She is the one
Her eyes, those eyes
All the time sparkled and commanded
I saw pain and desire at once

Her beauty was spellbound
Lust was in the air
I dipped and sank my soul
I gasped and panted
I was in a flame of her aura
I wrote, and wrote
A love letter
On the fire.

Poets Never Die

Poems are the voice of one's
Humans have voice
Poetry lives inside of all
But it does not sounds same

Poets do not have a quiet world,
On this roaring earth
They can't bury their words
Every word holds a meaning
Perhaps for someone or something
I believe the world of a poet is eternal
Somewhere the poets know
They will never die
Poets live
Forever until the end

The Winter Blue

After the colourful autumn
Neither the spiced pumpkin
Nor the happiness
Fits in my winter jar

The coldest winter
Came with the winter blue
Dark days were eating
The bright days
How am I supposed to
Look at the garden
Where Flowers disappeared like
My love

All of the sudden
There is the fragrance
The winter fragrance
Honeysuckle bloomed
In the garden of my sorrow

Heart's desire brought hope
Even in the deep winter
I found a light and followed it
I fell, I fell in love with myself
I learned

Self-acceptance is the light
In all the darkness
And I stand here.

If My Windows Could Speak

The darkness in the room
Made me fearful
There was something
Only I could see
The place was completely
Devoid of life

I looked at the sky
I failed to remember
Everything
If my windows could speak
They would share an unusual story

Memories bled
My heart palpitated
Just a moment
I thought
I could not make it

Unspoken words
No one would ever know
If my windows could speak
They would share an unusual story

I Do Not Care

I have a bear
Bear has no pair
It likes a hare
Hare has no ear
It is not fair

There is a sculpture
It has no structure
Once I take a picture
It looks bizarre
Things are not clear
It it so rare and
I do not care

We stuck together

Neither strangers nor lovers
Yet, we stuck together
Now and then
It offered a chat
I refused

 I carried a lot
It controlled a lot
A familiar silence remained
Yet we stuck together

Once, unbearable ache
Begun to drown
Dread of death
Fear of separation
A feeling of heaviness and
The grief and the sadness

Moments of confusion
once i wished this
I closed my eyes
Flash of favourite faces
"Please do not let me go"
I cried out loud

And in the end
I heard a whisper
It softly said
I got you
At last i felt for my heart.

Was It A Dream?

I never believed in love
Yet on a Saturday night
Like a sparking light
U came and hold my hand
And you made me believe in love

We walked on the cold street
We looked at the sky
Light shone in our heart
A smile on your face
And you gave me a gaze

How could I?
Forget all of these,
How could you?
Forget all of these

A day or a night
You made it the best
Your leafy eyes
Stole all of breath
You blew my mind
With your rosy lips
It tasted like

My better life
We danced till the night die

You chose me to love
You made me to love you
Once i started loving you
you walked away from my eyes

In a heartbeat
You dropped out of my sight
Was it a moment or
Was it a dream?
I never knew
I never knew you.

The Picturesque Pentland

A strange sense of peace
Spread from a wonderful place
It is wild and kind
It gives you the world
Indeed for the mood

Along the way
The dancing trees
Rushing river
Scurrilous squirrel
Wet mud smell
Eventually, It amuses you
Even in your bittersweet

A way to unwind
It makes your path
Deeper into the woods
Higher into the sky
From one month to another
Gradually seasons change
The hill stands silently in the background
And i call it the Picturesque Pentland

The Pain Is Only Mine

A farewell to my pain is a daydream
All pain kissed on the same place
My heart does not speak
It bleeds words for me
Those words are untold
Perhaps we do not share
the same language
I tried to learn
But failed miserably

The war took the first step
Many moons ago,
It is between my pain and I
Somebody said
Winner of the battle live
I still live
Since the pain is only mine

Hold that feeling

It was dark and a scary night
A mid night walk to the ocean
Once i joined the waves
Ocean wind gave me
An invisible wing

As time went by
The starry moon rose over the ocean
I looked at the moon
It gave me accompany
Glowing moon made my cold heart shone

I was too soft,
what made me heartless
A personal apologies to myself
Oh, hold that feeling
I smiled and smiled
Not anymore

The Door Opens at Midnight

There is a doorway
It is sacred
It opens At the midnight
Late night stillness
Makes it deep

There is something about the door
It opens for you, for me
And for all
When it opens it shows
Naked souls with genuine
thoughts and desires

There is something about the door
it is inevitable
It makes us a frequent visitor
A secret rendezvous
Our late night thoughts

I will See You Again

I can not tell you the reason
Why do I disappear
Like your missing socks
I want you to know
My roadway is
the worst way
And my travel is unravel

I can not tell you how
 my skin feels
Still the pain is unknown
There was a time
I wasn't acting
We could live
But we unlived

Now i can tell you
As time slips by
I will see you again
In my blue dreams

I Never Missed You

The morning sunlight never told me
To look for you
My morning coffee mug
never checked for yours
The jazz bar
Never brought your memories

The smell of the spring
Taste of the honey
The sounds of the waves,
Daylight, moonlight
Nothing missed you

Each step in the old town
My shadow never cried for you
I never searched your face in the crowd
I never looked back when i heard your name
I never fascinated by your remembrance
Nevertheless, if you asked my walls
They would whisper your name
Yet, i never missed you

The Finest Wine

A glass of the finest wine
Every sips
I tasted your lips
Unwanted thoughts
Squeezed my heart
I wanted to give you
A piece of my heart
A part you killed

Was that you or my wine ?

Late night gave
Unknown awkward
A cruel tear
I was unable to think
I am unexplainable
A bottle of the finest wine
No one can deny
My wine is feminine

The Way Things Are

The usual walks on
the Monday mornings
A sense of dread spread
All over the world
Races of mankind

That's how the way things are

People let you down
Don't let you fall
Don't let you fail
Everyone everywhere
Shares a common destiny

That's just the way things are

Mankind is in a mission
With tangle of questions
Time passes people fade
Remember that
Life in an open world
You are under surveillance

Middle Of Nowhere

I still rise
Middle of nowhere
With so many questions
There is a pressure
It pushes me to move forward
But I have so many questions

I still rise in
Middle of nowhere
Reality stays stressful
Truth hides inside
Doubts are a heavy burden
The chaotic world
Shows me dramatic souls
I am ever seeking, a tiny creation
Pure and untainted

www.ingramcontent.com/pod-product-compliance
Lightning Source LLC
LaVergne TN
LVHW021341200726
843509LV00014B/2612